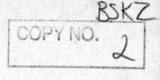

SABINE WICHERT

TIN DRUM COUNTRY

SALMON POETRY

Published in 1995 by
Salmon Publishing Ltd,
Upper Fairhill, Galway

© Sabine Wichert 1995

28/2/96

The moral right of the author has been asserted

The Publishers gratefully acknowledge the support of
The Northern Ireland Arts Council

A catalogue record for this book is available from the British Library

ISBN 1 897648 29 4

Cover illustration by Sue Smickler
Cover design by Poolbeg Group Services Ltd
Set by Poolbeg Group Services Ltd in Palatino 11/14
Printed by Colour Books, Baldoyle Industrial Estate, Dublin 13

To the memory of my father

Acknowledgements

Some of these poems have been previously published in *The Irish Press, Poetry Ireland Review, Fortnight, The Honest Ulsterman, Filmdirections, A Tribute to Bill Wiser, Raven Introductions 5, Cyphers, Outlines, Sparerib, Orbis, Gown Literary Supplement, The Sunday Tribune, Poetry Nottingham,* and *The Salmon.*

Many of these poems were written at the Tyrone Guthrie Centre, Annaghmakerrig. Special thanks therefore to the Irish Arts Councils and to Bernard and Mary Loughlin.

Contents

The Baptism
(Bonn, 15th February 1987 – for Felix and Marco)

Their grandfather came from Danzig,
and Poland is never quite lost;
no need to hold these in arms:
they are ten and four years old,
they want to be christened.

'Work may not get you anywhere':
the minister's sermon on unemployment
in an affluent Church, the hymns
confirm: by mercy only. I'm present
under false pretences; God is still

a trusted castle here, as Luther
proclaimed, the Thirty Years' War
has yet to happen, the music
strong as the words, to help
survive in darker times.

These boys will not be unemployed,
caught safely in the net of European
middle classes, from Ireland to Greece.
Will they want faith? I haven't been
on terms with any God for many years,

yet promise to be their spiritual guide.
What will they choose between the ego and the rest,
where will they settle, in castles or flats,
with hymns, computers, paintings, or books,
in Belfast, Athens, Bonn, or Gdansk?

Memory

The shadow moves slowly
across the pavement.
Who was the man
on whose bed
I spent last night,
talking and unaware?

There are no gods,
the magic is in us,
and we to be blamed
for all authority.

The milkman passed
many hours ago.
A night of brutal sentiment,
and somewhere truth:
the missing sunshine present
in the shadows of conversation.

A word touched and a thought,
the air was stale and full of smoke,
and when I left I knew
I should have stayed.

Fragile February

Colours on paper
when a blade of grass
is more determined.

An uncertain centre
and unanswered questions.

How long, for instance,
will the grass hold the soil
while water burrows
underneath near the substance?

The sun will pierce
the Valentines,
the colours change,
the form remains
but meanings do not
meet between
the old ways and
their new conceptions.

3

Small Things

These get me down today:
a face in a passing car,
a signature in a visitors' book,
a supermarket trolley.

When I smoke
I do not dare
to touch my lips
yet I smoke and smoke.

Even the grass
outside the window
grows at an alien angle.

I wish I knew
how to use
a knife properly.

Perhaps then I could cut
through the news and the power
and find a way.

The Torso

A dark and dull morning,
after the rain all night,
even pulling the curtains
doesn't give much more light;
the air is heavy,
all lamps still on,
something threatens,
something hides,
the cat is alert and electric;
conversations turn to
heart attacks and angina pectoris;
someone says, having seen
one museum, you've seen them all,
and others hold this true
for landscapes, too:
but when I go out
for a walk in the dripping wet,
I see a tree trunk turn into a body:
perfectly concentrated and self-contained,
luminous in the undergrowth.

Communications

No difficulty in meeting
the black and yellow skin,
talking to faces denoting
mainly different culture.

Between the droning helicopter's perpetuity
and the policeman's secretive call,
what strangely showed as alienation
of difference in similarity –

The shock: used to understand,
make allowances, be humble,
or arrogant, where difference occurs,
accepting the line between word and deed.

Cut up, sliced into chronology
you encounter in some nights the bridge
over the cultural gap you never knew
existed, meet strangers, communicate.

It hit when you found
you could not reach your neighbour,
or climb the low fence:
living or understanding.

You thought you touched strange countenance
in reassuring confirmation: humanity achieved.
Yet precious connections broke like spiders' webs
on impact with the mess of life.

Adjust your bias: the letter arrived
after you had resigned yourself to fever
and the sirens of ambulances; it briefly
gave answers and filled the void.

Easter Monday in Belfast

Rain falls on the cut tulips for sale
at the City Hall. While trees begin
to green, the marching season has begun:
my expensive strawberries bleed into the cream.

The yellows and pinks of suburbia's
well-tended front gardens, and yet
the feudal-fascist perversion: they
own the soil spiritually, they say, my
back garden is only a saleable commodity:

it was violated again last night. Someone
walked over the daffodils, cut himself
on the gorse and broke a fence which
I'll have to replace by barbed wire.

A Job in Town

Not bad, really. Keeps you in bread and butter,
healthy, too, nicely balanced between desk and building site
and no one much bothers you.

Weeds have started to take over and even the dogs
grow lazy and we get bored, too, sometimes when
it rains all day.

You have to stay in the hut then, play cards, read the comics,
as we are not to enter the building, too dangerous and
there is also a legal hitch somewhere.

They brought bombs in here several times; two years ago
the management gave up, even though there is plenty left
                                                    standing,
and we took over.

Sometimes it's really nice, there are eight of us, we
work shifts, sit in the sun, read the papers, feed the dogs,
chat: someone is always unhappy.

Monday Jim had trouble at home, but we had
sorted it out by the time he had to go; yesterday it
was all about Bill's parents:

They are waiting for the government's money to come
                                                    through
to rebuild the shop; much nicer it will be, too, chemist
mind you, small town.

Nobody wants to buy this place, not surprising if you ask me, it's very big and they'd just bring more bombs; it looks very grand, especially burning.

Visitors, Co. Monaghan

A German professor called
on his holiday tour,
attracted to the house set
by the lake.

When shown around, his
wife remarked upon
the beautiful proportions
of the rooms.

He saw the peace and quiet
and was much impressed:
how one could think in here
and write.

Educational medicine,
he said his subject was,
on which he thought
and wrote.

No, history did not
interest him, his work
was future orientated,
what next

to write and publish,
to debate and take
into account, science
marched forward.

He had just bought
a boat to take home
and have holidays with
in the future.

In an Irish House

This is your room,
the warmest in the house,
well sheltered
from the west wind:

I remember, the winds
of my childhood
always came from the East;

you could walk into them,
but few people did,
most sheltered, or ran;

few set sails against them
looking for a new life.

I like my protected room
looking onto a lake,
while windy deceptions
storm outside.

Conversation

How the unaffordable car insurance
wracked the morale of the country:
a strangely puritan gathering: no one present
had ever bought anything they couldn't pay for.

It reminded me of our concert –

Everyone else in the country was cheating:
even the nuns found ways to avoid VAT,
there was little left to hold on to.

 – we had taken the interval on the roof
to find a sheltered smoke by the chimney.

Labour, and money, and resources,
relations between debts and desires –

The sad trombone came through the window
as we lit up, hands briefly touching,
eyes averted as soon as they met –

small scale innocent householding.

My memories of Lough Neagh and your
mirrors could never have paid the taxes
on our Van Gogh and Miles Davis,
but we didn't know then, or later.

By the Fireside

The trees stand ready for the spring
which will not come this year,
it's snow instead, and hail again.

The library is heavy with mostly Irish
lives and times, its references branch
into the English classics, politics and history.

The corridors' photos and ghosts: condemned
to the eternity of the moment, heroes and criminals,
thrown up by the see-saw of history

which circumvents circumstances, short-circuits
intentions, haunts through pens and pages,
types its message on the fire-screen:

no Arcadia; here too, people are frightened,
need enemies for their identity; you don't know
will they murder where the talk is murderous.

If you only read between your own lines
the beam remains a mote, pleasantly blurred,
your insecurities gain firmness: even timid souls

grow imperialist under threat: reason only works
from a distance: foresight, hindsight, a tool
for historians, with little place in history.

When the stag meets the butterfly, there is little room for manoeuvre, but you can preserve some of their beauty: a pin into a cushion, antlers up against the wall.

The Building Site

The land slopes
gently to the Lagan:
are all our houses
built on stilts?

Look how the glasses
rattle on their shelves,
how cracks appear
in unexpected corners.

They build new houses
and secure the ground
by ramming steel poles
into the earth.

Will this prevent
a slide, when with
each stroke the hammer
strikes the windows

up the hill protest,
and doors shake
quietly, and slowly,
turn by supple turn

screws unwind steadily?
My double-glazing
even, meant to keep
the outside there,

begins to echo
and reverberate
and feels less safe
with every blow.

15

Only the Sky

The irate young painter was
perhaps a little jealous:
why don't you show some concern
in your work, in what surrounds you,
the suffering, the way people walk
and live and experience?

On the white wall hung a painting:
a tree, oddly out of place:
its healthy branches, broad-leaved,
seemed transported from a park;
it stood on a grassy patch
just a few yards from the sea.

But this society is rotten,
the established abstractionist
replied in helpless irritation,
and as the sun broke into the room,
someone else said, only the sky
is without limits in Ireland.

The late afternoon glided
over the walls, the picture;
the early autumn sky stretched in
bands and bands of shades of blues
and greys and greens, over small
hills, lakes, places and people.

Of Vistula and Lagan

When I was born
they had just
liberated the land
from alien possession.
Where I was born
ownership of land
was much disputed.

I inherited
the burning cities
of Europe,
the pulped flesh
and distorted minds,
and always
the marching boots:
mine, mine, mine.

When I was born
my father's name
had just
been changed
to sound more German.
Where I was born
nations were at war.

Human material
was in vogue,
skin cheap,
people glanced

over their shoulder
before confirming
nationhood
in blood and soil.

So I learnt
that names
don't matter,
and land
doesn't belong,
that roots grow
in many soils,

and power
is dangerous
in any hand,
politician's,
priest's or poet's;
that many rivers
flow across
one latitude.

Restraints

The thought of a beautiful life
in the boxes of blooming geraniums
edging the balcony of a two-room
flat on the second floor:

these, and the hills on the horizon:
perhaps sheep are grazing there,
and couples picking flowers in white,
having all day to dream in.

The crumbling cottage in the centre
of bog-centuries, the fire soaring,
the smells of rain and shelter,
sheep and some lost birds.

Somewhere the ocean promises
the life of towns one always wanted
for one's children, able to choose
boxes and geraniums on window-sills.

Zorba Revisited

I went again not resisting
the memory: joy, life
and dance, sun and tenderness,
the acceptance seemed natural.

What I found now was
the bent knee's hysteric inevitability
and no reassurance.

There are battlefields,
sad rebellions, against stones
and trees that rarely grow.

I thought Zorba was life,
but these grey Athenian streets
promise nothing.

Rational

This strange reluctance
to be glad when once
again a countryman ejaculates
while climbing up Acropolis.

This strange delight
upon a warden's cry
that I could only be
a Swedish girl come South.

And quiet fury
when the man from Crete
extolled the wonders of
the Germans and their history.

Ascending the Parthenon
has its delights even at noon,
yet I'd rather be, any time
and place, one of the locals.

Or, well, the Swedes did
not damage mankind much
of late, no need to feel guilty;
perhaps I'd opt for that after all.

Of Earaches and Contact Lenses
(for Medbh and Hugh)

No words or syrup will cure your earache,
these palliatives for loneliness when you can't
squeeze in between your brothers, sleeping
                                        entangled,
locked together like lens and eyeball,
almost one: to enhance vision, clarify the world,
make it palatable; even when your mother,
your white witch mother, has the magic. Listen.

One late September our bus broke down
on the hills a couple of miles outside
Delphi: we were a conservative party,
the driver a communist who swore gently
at the engine and waved us away.

We were going home and to appease
the gods we performed Apollo's
rites at the wrong time of the year,
sweating in the dust by the roadside,
garlands of weeds, crowns, the sun,

our back to the mountains, lonely
with goodbyes, no more contact lens
closeness: a taxi came to fetch
him out of the dance to the airport.
Later we sat by the village cypresses

eating feta and drinking wine sadly
among whirlwinds of Greek political
conversations, waiting for our bus
to recover, the gods to forgive us,
remembering yesterday and the days before

when they counted the number of households,
the sex of all inhabitants,
the number of children under fifteen
and of servants and lodgers
in each quarter of the town.

You are not yet fifteen, and you have your
mother's magic, your drawings as lenses, your
sophisticated faces on child-like bodies looking
askance at the world. By and by your earache
will go, you'll no longer notice, and you'll
like the present long after you'll have discovered
the future or all the dangers of the past.

Alluvium

Do you think Zurich, for instance –
wrote Benn, and was right;

and yet it's not age that matters,
nor the exotic places' allure;

it is the customs and habits
of strange places and people

that make you aware of yourself;
and what they wash up and deposit

cannot be known by thinking
and learning, however Kantian.

Ararat Perhaps
(for Sophie)

We haven't seen the peaks
since we left the Ark.
Are we still hoping to get
back there some time,

to the sweet-scented arabis
on the slopes in summer,
to a symbol of unity,
love and survival?

Is that enough to appease
the vishaps and gain
the shabapets' protection, when
golden hills no longer shine?

What would we have done
about Jews, gypsies, and
dissidents, if we are afraid
to ring the dogwarden in case

a neighbour will get a fine?
The postman brought me a new
request to declare why I don't pay
for the television I do not watch.

We register the noise, but are
too liberal to complain; the sun
doesn't pass us by, but
the dark clouds do: we only

see their silver lining; no
informers we, we want to be
loved and survive, not to
see any writing on walls.

Perhaps out of the hollow stalk
that issued us after smoke
and flame and exiled us for good,
new and fresh colours will come.

Sometimes in that far corner
of my garden where no Mediterranean
sun will ever reach, something
meets in contrast: the deepest

blue of the sky and clean cotton
white clouds, the varied greens
of oak and lilac against
the fragile brown of a dying branch.

The Itch
(for Felix and Marko)

I surprised a couple of deer:
high grass almost hid
their jumping free and fleeing.

My nephews would race them,
wild grandsons of my father:
he runs in them, born late.

He grew up in Tin Drum country;
those boys will not stop
growing or cease running.

After the deer a stranger:
well known, it turns out,
grasping fame and complaining:

how money and reputation
had brought the itch,
had damaged family and life.

My father's visions grew sour
with polio at twelve,
his wildness suppressed,

invalidated into history; later
he tried hard not to convey
his dreams to his unruly children.

The stranger walked on,
rushing to work for his debts
and the expensive flat in the city.

The deer stopped at the forest,
looked back to watch my moves,
and then began to graze.

When I think of those boys,
I, too, feel itchy, fail to settle,
expect to be disturbed.

Relief

Outpatients all,
we queue on comfortable chairs,
nervous and private, not showing
that our wounds need licking.

One came out once
in tears, a battered face
and greyer hair, it should not
come so late in life.

This one came smilingly:
I'll have it out,
she said, better one healthy
and alive to raise it.

The one in the blue sweater
behind me had laser treatment
once a month and did not
want to know her chances:

she refused information
and thought her nerves
were better off in ignorance
than too much knowledge.

When my turn came
my cells had beaten
the intruder, appeased, until
next time perhaps or never.

Departure

Every day I picked some blackberries on my walks,
they now begin to taste musty and stale. It is time.

The trees begin to develop new personalities after a dull,
wet summer: green, yellow, red, orange, and brown.

Every leaf stands to attention today, hardly a ripple
on the surface of the lake: a motionless, very erect
   landscape.

When I have a map, I know where I am: distinguish
distances, straight lines and circles, triangles even.

Many of these ways are not routes, leading nowhere,
or uncharted: how they relate and meet each other.

The sky, as if painted with too much opaque white
to hard-edge the clouds; difficult to find images there.

One loses out – wedged between ladies and girls:
woman walking in set scenery, not clueless,

yet hesitant to ask for the cork-screw or a pint,
while willing to stroke the cat and go with the seasons.

When I turn back at the gate for a final glance,
I see a blackberry gleam: fully ripened, wet and dark.

Christmas '80
(for Anna Stewart)

The sun walked in surprisingly
at midday, waking the dust
which was bedding quietly
upstairs until spring, but
she closed the blinds to keep
the spirits by the fire.

Handel washed softly
over toy delights and
a cooking turkey allowed
the voices to insist
and press and break.

Paintings, publishers, and investments,
all in the washing up; jokes
ready to jump out of solid wood
by the staircase, like brandy
over the pudding easy to ignite,
like the sons' witty innocence.

When it broke, it was
a flicker only, a glance,
a touch of maternity,
a widowed eye,
a hand touching tomorrow.

In the Ladies

Down well carpeted steps,
behind plush doors,
through mirror reflected passages
to the heart of the matter:

here they sit smoking in front of mirrors
and talk and laugh as if
this was their aim in coming,
to enjoy themselves down here,

not their men upstairs,
the drink, the music or dancing,
while they remake their faces:
mascara doesn't really matter;

it's like washing up, it has
to be done; but here is warmth
where upstairs is cold competition.
Between these plush stools

something comes true
as in kitchens over cups of tea,
not in the limelight above
where dresses and eyes are lit.

Easter at Ailesbury Grove
(for Ailbhe)

The train that brought me here
searched for escapes in rivers,
trees and travel, childish memories
on literary pages under whitish sky.

This courtyard lets the child
play in the sun and concentrates
the presence on Lydia:
this is bearable, the protected light
tempts me to settle with myself.

On Reconstruction

Brecht's plum tree could bear fruit here:
through Georgian windows we look at
Bloomsbury Square, leaves scamper like
flocks of birds chasing Virginia's ghost,
the square's trees tinged with autumn colours.

We've come to talk history. In plushy seats
and slightly overfed we consider the aftermath
of war, the reconstruction of what had been
a fascist state. Is what survives innocuous,
like leaves and birds, or does it guarantee us

worse to come: white clouds with dark bellies,
easy to perceive and difficult to grasp.
We try to understand what always just escapes,
chasing facts and counter-facts, never unpacking,
ready for late-night sessions over pizzas,

typewriters, and shared clues and insights,
rarely opening windows to let the fumes escape,
as artists might have to after using spray-paints.
The pictures on our walls need to be
straightened, again and again. Each room

is different, if only in the shades of white
on its walls, in too much dusting, or too little,
in too many plants, or too few. Light falls
on the chandeliers in this Georgian drawing room.
I try to imagine: Brecht meeting Virginia Woolf.

After the Sabbatical

After a year in libraries and archives,
of resting his mind and letting
his thought loose on hundreds of books
and authors, he thought he had found
something new and important, about
time and power and human deliberations,
something about the dynamics of change.

He returned in hope, to communicate,
stimulate, teach, and sit on committees –

The first meeting was called at very short
notice for an uncivilised hour
in a place now called cost-centre 15 B
in which his unit, 36 c, was to debate
whether it should be large A or a
small a Department: financial planning
notions and unit-costs soon juggled
with fading memories of yellowing pages.

He thought of resigning, but he was needed:
unit 36 c could not do without his insights.

Collective Guilt
(for Lior)

It was a dull room where
they lived among students
that summer, but air-conditioned,
while the sun beat the tarmac outside.

I'd quite forgotten he said while they ate,
that you are German, I a Jew.
She edged away sensing the burden,
feeling history's responsibility.

O please, he said,
we don't want any sacrifices,
let's keep it personal.

The blank walls made her
uneasy yet; it was hot
that August in Texas, and Israel
no further away than Auschwitz.

Hesitant Visit Home

Perhaps some battles were won:
there is milk and honey now;
that must be the Eden they always wanted,
secretly; but is the volcano dead –
it still rumbles inside me.

I do not trust this history,
something might crumble any day;
it is too calm: a new landscape
might settle, but the picture seems
to hang in the wrong frame.

They seem so content and relaxed;
tired perhaps, or even tranquil.
They are still struggling, but with much
less effort now, taking fairy tales in their stride,
working to certain hours, then resting.

Shopping

I

Their good mornings
were once mine –
I no longer understand.

The neighbour expects
unknown things of me
and shopowners give me
puzzled looks.
I don't remember
what to say.

Wasn't it only yesterday
that I stood inhibited
by their demands?
They do it again,
they still restrict me,
I'm quite lost.

Strangely familiar gestures
which I cannot repeat,
cannot respond to:
half a pound of sugar, please,
and thank you, but even
that sounds wrong.

I'm of their mould,
but can't fit any longer,
it's closing in;
I want to run again
after only two days
of trying to be friendly.

II

The flavour of words comes back slowly,
the shy feeling for sentences,
if only after stumbling
in surprise over asking for five rolls.

It's all so obvious:
what could be more German
than that cream cake, Torte,
yet it sounds artificial.

You cannot yet join
in the easy chatter, self-conscious
even of saying thank you
too often, pronouncing it well.

You want to participate:
these are rather dear, that's a bargain,
those sausages look just right;
like a child trying your mother's tongue.

Your mind opens the gate,
lets phrases through readily,
the weight isn't right, though,
too little homely friendliness.

So easy to get lost
in the taste and tangle of language
on a shopping trip for five rolls
and some meat in your own tongue.

Architecture

There used to be holes
in this smooth lane,
to jump over, ride a bicycle through,
and broken fences' peeling paint.

The joy of climbing through that wall,
bricked up now.
What do they know?
We skated here in winter

and played the puddles in spring.
This intimacy defies
building programmes and cleaning-up campaigns:
we hid behind those damp corners

from each other, and things to come;
these mouldy wooden planks,
no longer there, but carried
in our luggage ever since.

Still Lives

The lane was still there,
behind the last houses of the town,
where we had yet
expected some answers
or at least escapes,
where meadows had stretched
and a clear road had lain ahead.

Now there were crows
over untended fields,
ready for building, not the plough,
and only a square board
with black official letters:
Beware of rabies.
Dogs to be kept on a lead.

Someone must have changed
our cards: we were so certain
we held all the trumps.

Aunt Else

In her seventies now, she still
dreams of tall handsome strangers
and reads only nice books:

predigested and not too many,
after the trouble she's seen
in her life's time of European history.

She travels even more now
that her pension allows exotic places
from bus windows and plushy hotels.

Her postcards always avoid
reality in favour of pleasant
weather and blue seas.

Not so surprising perhaps,
when she only just missed
the Siberian labour camps.

She likes beauty, and the cherry tree
in front of her window must blossom
on time, as the landlord is asked

to keep the heating up. Her retired
friends call at well appointed hours
and they are all happy together.

The Youngest Sister
(in memory of Lena)

The youngest of eight:
she looked delightful
on sepia bear skin:
a status symbol of her
upwardly mobile
working-class family,
with the advantage
of easy extra-superiority
feelings in a country
of two nations.

There are photos of her
as a young girl,
dressed in white,
holding a tennis racket
(more middle-class
paraphernalia) and later
holding her nieces and
playing with her nephews
as they arrived:
dark-eyed, full of hope.

Her father and the priest
showed her how to fit
into the order of things,
moulded her as a slave
into overlapping hierarchies;
and she loved it all,
learned quickly and for good;

only later her photos
took on that look of a
spaniel's submissiveness.

Respecting her older sisters
and brothers, as father
and mother, and state
authorities, she cooked
and cared and looked
forward to life, cooking
and caring. When the time
came her education
was enough to make her
a cashier in a shop.

She liked it and
worked conscientiously:
Prussian, Catholic, and secure,
hopeful and confident.
Her first batch of suitors
she dismissed as
not quite worthy enough.
Then there are
no photos
for a very long time:

history had caught
up with her, raped her
of her inheritance,
threw her among
strangers and strangeness,
yet forced her
to survive.

She now served her sisters,
deprived by war
of husbands and lovers.

She learned it had
been wrong to support
Hitler, that supermen
were not superior
to men, though
she was no mean
anti-Semite herself.
The Church survived,
but she often complained
how lax things were

and how people
no longer knew
right from wrong,
so that her family
became her true church,
until only one,
her closest sibling,
was left whom she
loved and cherished
and cleaned and cooked for.

When that one died,
her world collapsed:
no space left for dreams
or even hope. She briefly
moved to a married one
in Southern parts
who demanded

her service and
sent her back
when she fell ill:

she came back dying,
drinking and in despair,
not wanting to heal,
no point in recovery.
She died that summer
of broken hopes
and disappointed
of rewards
on a toilet seat
in a hospital.

Judgement in Newcastle, Co. Down

Neolithic savages
may have sharpened
their stones against
stones here, added
wood to harpoon
a dinner. We
have come to judge

the Young Film Critic
of the Year Competition.
The dark wild night
encircles the barricaded
hotel, follows us
over freshly laid concrete
and wooden planks,

leaves us in plush
cosiness to decide
who best assessed
The Mission or
Rambo, while
the storm does not
penetrate beyond

the searchlight outside.
We judge and eat,
and spill out
after the brandy
into the lit gales,
flooded car parks,
goodbyes

whipped
from our lips.
Through rain-
splashed glasses
I see the air
take my identity:
opened handbag

sheds
credit cards,
driving licence,
memberships,
me
into the rain.
I stand

lit up,
on stage, light-
hearted, heavy-footed
against the wind.
I want to make
a film about
Neanderthal man.

Providence Passing Through

In the early hours,
after too many drinks
and too much
intelligent conversation
his eyes had grown wet
with remorse:

Hitler died, he said,
from the shock of the gas bill,
the communists killed
because they believed
in themselves and a future
of happiness.

All lost lives
behind closed doors,
and the world's guilt
on his shoulders.
The wind did not subside
that night.

A few bombs exploded,
his misery
was enhanced by Guinness.
All betrayed love
on the last plane
to Tel Aviv.

Bad Timing
(for B.)

The blood pulses and trickles –
it might have been perfect.
The ambulance rushes on:
not even daring to hold hands in the dark,
watching love turn into possession,
wanting to own too much,
wanting to love too much –
it could have been perfect.

Empty-handed,
heads under water,
giving and giver destroyed.
Flakes of memory, storms
of equal vice:
love and possession,
fragile snow, spots of rust –
it needn't always be murder
but often is.

No takers for Mucha and Klimt
hanging lost between Fidelio's last chords.
The greens and yellows had only slowly
come into our conversations,
attacking the reds and white,
blending the black and greys.
When the lights go up
you have to go home.
No time for giving –
it could have been perfect.

Reading Kafka's Letters

The pain and fear in every sentence,
the insight, too, that things will last
but not enough to suffer
just this one life.

Mice and children, journeys even
became fearful, to be avoided
by order of malfunctioning lungs
and a despairing heart.

Each sentence so carefully handled,
a sculptor's work, you no longer feel
where the chips fell as form emerged,
and so little considered finished.

The perfection that wanted to burn
all this perfection as no little
workshop in Palestine could be forthcoming
and protein and ozone were not enough.

While Reading Sartre

We love our friends badly –
it's all
we can do
between the first tooth
and the last.

Love
excluded by other
and self,
lost in words,
rarely rescued.

It was easier
and more difficult
before
the link between
act
and reflection.

Now one
is one,
just,
yet still
the other
and oneself.

If love
is what
remains
there might
still be
a future,

while there is
choice
and decision
and a few
friends
poorly loved.

Charlotte Brontë

You, too, must have known
that the gods are merciless,
yet you spilt your sisterly love
and rejected
the reason around you.

You could not endure
that life has no answers
and braced the moors
to feed your imagination
on roses and sentiment.

Perhaps you could not,
given the circumstances,
see beyond the graveyard
in front of your door,
or only too much.

You, sister, were cautious and demure,
where greener grass could not be raised,
and your clouds obscured
what might after all have been
a life impossible to live.

The Assessors

The assessors came, uninvited.
Or had we asked them by implication?
They wouldn't say what they were to estimate.
The water was still, a breezeless mirror
of more uniform greens and first signs of colour.

Was our price too high for not selling ourselves?
Had they come to cost our worth
or the quality of our surroundings?
Were we rateable by their standards,
could we be punished for our innocence?

Perhaps they'd come for the dying season:
counting the squirrels, roughly one and a half
per mile, driven to mash, or the stiff
hares thrown onto the roadside?
Was a headcount required after all?

There had been shooting too, continued
intermittently, day and night.
Were they commissioned to supervise,
to evaluate: death and the artist,
compelled to find inexorable connections?

They may also have seen
the ever growing flock of birds
assembling over the lough
in more structured formation each evening,
as if debating whether it was time yet

to leave, like words in a poem
not quite ready for flight.
But we didn't hurt animals –
we admired their states when alive
and later ate them, reverently.

The assessors had come from
across the border in flashier cars
than we had seen for weeks.
The deaths remained unexplained though,
and they were investigating us, not accidents.

Were we their game then, or their gamble,
were we responsible for them?
Was our secluded naïvety indictable,
had we allowed something to happen,
without intent, were we to blame?

Nobody but Michaelangelo could
have painted the Sistine Chapel – *
weren't we in our right then,
way-worn with concentration
and recreational walks?

They chatted amiably enough
while we gave them lunch.
The next day the fishermen had gone
from the shore and we found
a dead fox by the wayside.

*paraphrased after Henry Moore

The Poet's Research Assistant

Today she asked me to find
a word-field 'round wrath,
to go beyond Roget's Thesaurus
and include associations
she might have made when
having related experiences.

An easy assignment compared
with her moody days when I hover
without having access to her
and her mind. It's her fault
if she excludes me. How can I
help if left out of the picture?

Most of my time is spent
in libraries, or just keeping
my senses attuned, ready to guide
her when she comes back
from her walks, exhausted,
open to suggestions, exhilarated,

prepared for word-painting
and deeper layers of insight.
Today's emerging poem appears
to be about a woman and her cat
called Wanda who live
in a third floor Pimlico flat.

Sometimes the cat preens herself
in the sun on the window-sill
and people look up and feel dizzy.
Sometimes the woman leans out
crooning Waanda, Waanda, or sharper
Wanda, Wandaa, in a moaning

yet lean voice, knowing the cat
will be back, if she goes on
calling her – in days, in weeks perhaps,
or months. Waandaa. All
my work on anger and hate
seems to have ended in this soft call.

Oasis

Step softly beneath
these ancient plane trees,
unexpected
in this bleak stretch
of grey rocks
and browning grass.

Gently bend your face
to the quietly running
water between these stones,
come to rescue
only these roots.

Don't rush,
I beg you,
don't be surprised,
be easy, and drink.

Misguided

It is dull and wet
as I drive back
after a fog-frozen night.

Turn right after the river,
the AA-man had advised,
then straight, over two crossroads,
sharp left, then right again.

I watch leaves depart
from trees, turning darker
as they fall, and I wonder
why a strange town felt
home after a few hours:

how little we talked,
the careful deliberation
of not touching even clothed
parts of each other,
the Kentucky-Fried Chicken,
the only meal we shared,

eaten in the front of the car:
eyes parallel, no conversation;
what is it that I like
about you still? I felt
at home. But now?

I've missed the river, there
are no crossroads here
and I don't know where
the car is taking me.

Weathered

We talk too much,
you and I.
You look
out of the window
for hours,
self-contained,
and then
mention the weather.
I ask you
whether the milkman
has been paid;
and all this time
rain drips
down the gutter
into the brickwork.
We talk too much,
you and I.

Mourning

I, too, was afraid of the dark,
and there was to be no light,
but the dark never came;
it was light and without burden:
there was a bed but no sleep,
there was no bed but trees remained.

So I cried, so what,
so I started to mourn,
forgetting the past,
the future deprived.

No silver lining, only a cloud.
It will go. Something happened:
nothing happened and that was important.

The trees were bursting their buds prematurely.
You didn't have to bring that chill wind.
These things don't happen twice.

We are so privileged,
sadness in our drinks
but a breast to rest on
even in mourning.

Bitterness: there is a door
somewhere, but it might
remain closed to our knock.

The fight is over, another begun,
discard the pieces, find again,
repair the brazen tomorrow.

Bondage

The dragonflies danced on the window-sill,
fighting, or making love, I could not tell –
when your car drove by and stopped.

Your business, as ever opaque, made me forget
the insects, expelled me, to crush the path,
to take revenge for your temerity and my tenacity.

How oblique had been my umbrage before;
now it could not be tamed: it hated
the trees, shyly beginning to colour,

the wet, long grass slashing my legs,
and the fungi-smelling woods.
There were no fish where I crossed the stream.

But your presence lingered, as it had for years,
malignant and inescapable. The window
was open when I returned, the dragonflies gone.

Bucephalus

A cloud over the lough, a wind,
a shower: news in the Sahara,
he said, but not news here.

We were extracting meaning
from facts of history
and talked about the weather:
safe, but requiring strength
I do not always possess.

Time was yesterday –
then the pendulum stopped:

the Thracian favourite
rides through memory
waking the banshee.

The farmer's spirited cows
escaped this morning into the spring,
bucking wildly, embracing
air, space and time.

On the lake the little people appear
with white beards and earlocks.
Tilly Losch raises her arms
in front of the mirror,
her hands ready to dance.

The two ancient trees in front of the house
whisper 'til late at night,
when Alexander's horse
charges into the forest;
the white cats are hiding,
their litters censored.

She just couldn't handle
that much freedom,
the American writer had said,
and I had wondered
what this new liberty was
that needed so much practice.

Nothing is ever lost:
some hand is forced
to catch it, some cell
retain it, and slowly,
slowly the tender pendulous clock
begins to count again,
purloining meaning from life.

Letter from A.

Harmonies and cacophonies
drove me under the stairs,
helped me master technology
to hear: you are lonely, sitting
and waiting for food and company.

You smell Homer and me
and you lift your head
and scream, staring blindly,
fighting nature still:
we call it mourning.

There is a tree outside my window
branching and branching like Eve,
with a single bird sitting
large and dark against the sky:
a romantic painting.

We are twigs, at the end
of a shoot, stretching towards
the sun, throwing reflections
onto the lake, staring
into the distance above the clouds.

One should be blindfolded
and smell the springs of childhood,
getting lost again among
too many long legs.
All dogs are lame here.

The big cats helped me
to light a fire against the cold:
they are gentle and full of strange
thoughts, and their noise reverberates
in my brain, and I miss you.

Rituals of death, they say,
are vital for survival,
nice funerals good for the soul.
Ours was impromptu:
tears, pain, and revulsion,

and we did not really believe
he was dead. All roads here
lead back into themselves,
however often they cross each
other on their way; and I walk

and walk and then, fall down
the precipice; I didn't know
I was lonely, lonelier almost
than you. It's called Newbliss,
like a mispronunciation of nubilous.

While Münzenberg is trying to save
the revolution of fifty years ago,
a red-sweatered boy leans
against the grey wall, quietly
watching the sun warm the stone.

It is much noisier here than at home:
building work, engines, children,
and someone says, Sibelius was
really romantic, the piano next door,
people chatting: the cows need milking.

The milk of childhood
and Stalin's interest in Spain,
and why should quiet landscape
be so green and so intense,
intrude and explode yesterday's heroes?

They're mixing cement like dough,
and birds, your size, good mouthfuls,
sky-dive for morsels left by the dogs.
The new studios will be ready
when summer arrives with the painters.

The poetry of trees and mathematics:
that summer graveyard was hot
as they burnt him to ashes,
and I came home to you crying,
remember, and you cried, too.

A little girl in a bright red dress
plays with a big black umbrella,
too large to hold, a perfect home,
dark clouds scatter hail,
and she runs: red against green.

And then these other battlefields,
not the Aragon front and not
those of the mind or the News of the World:
there are two who hold hands
and have that sheepish look:

they walk and talk and
make me jealous, their
secret touches spice the air;
their silences are real, but not
yet perfect; they may need time.

Wait for me on the landing
as you always do. I'll bring
spiced air and more time;
you'll have to be quiet, and I
will be patient and understand.